COPING WITH LOSS AND GRIEF

GEOFFREY GLASSOCK and
MEGAN GRESSOR

ROBINSON
London

Robinson Publishing Ltd
7 Kensington Church Court
London W8 4SP

First published in Great Britain by
Robinson Publishing Ltd 1995

Published in Australia as *Living with Loss & Grief* by
Gore & Osment Publications Pty Ltd

Copyright © Megan Gressor 1992
Copyright © Gore & Osment Publications Pty Ltd

ISBN 1–85487–384–9

A copy of the British Library Cataloguing in Publication
data is available from the British Library

Note
This book is not a substitute for your doctor's or health
professional's advice, and the publishers and authors
cannot accept liability for any injury or loss to any
person acting or refraining from action as a result of the
material in this book. Before commencing any health
treatment, always consult your doctor.

Printed and bound in the EC

Contents

Chapter 1
The Many Faces of Grief

Grief is one of the few certainties in life, like death and taxes. It is also one which our hedonistic society tends to keep under wraps, which means that many of us are unable to cope when loss occurs. Such unpreparedness can prolong the mourning process, making it even more painful.

There are many types of bereavement. The one which usually springs to mind is loss of a loved one – the death of a spouse, parent, child, sibling or friend. This can cause the most intense grief, because it is so very final.

It is widely recognised that events like divorce and miscarriage also provoke strong grief reactions. But there are other types of loss which take a toll, like disability; such things as disfigurement, blindness, amputation, infertility, failing memory and loss of independence all cause us to grieve. So do social events, such as losing a job or a friendship.

These things affect how we see ourselves and the world, and we mourn for what has gone. Change itself is a form of loss, but many people don't understand why they feel upset at such apparently positive events as moving home, travelling, getting married or starting a new job.

It is now realised that trauma victims – such as hostages, witnesses of massacres or survivors of catastrophic events – experience their own form of grief, which can be quite debilitating. There is also 'disenfranchised grief' – mourning that is made harder by going unacknowledged by others. For example, the emotions of partners of AIDS victims, or couples who have split after a long established relationship, are just as involved as their 'official' counterparts (heterosexual partners, divorcing couples). But society does not grant there grief the same status, or concede that it exists at all.

The expression of grief is just as diverse. Some people 'pretend' that the loss hasn't happened. Others talk and cry incessantly. Withdrawal, depression and sickness are common symptoms of grief, as are feelings of guilt and anger. Some people, bewildered by the strength of their own feelings, fear they are going mad.

It doesn't help that many onlookers shy away from expressions of grief, which can leave mourners in a sort of limbo, feeling lonely and isolated. As the saying goes, 'Weep and you weep alone'.

But mourners are not alone. Bereavement is a universal experience and grief is a normal part of life – not a very comfortable or pleasant one – but one which must be experienced, not denied.

It is important that people mourning any sort of loss, from the major to the seemingly trivial, understand that their feelings are not a sign of sickness or instability.

The pain of loss will eventually heal, and may even have some positive aspects, such as the opportunity for personal growth. It can force people to reassess what's important in their lives, and that usually turns out to be the quality of their relationships with others.

The better people understand the bereavement process, the better they will be able to cope with loss. This book is intended to assist in that understanding.

Chapter 2
The Stages of Grief

There are many responses to grief, and each person reacts in an individual manner. Some people seem better able to cope than others, whose sense of loss may be unresolved for years. In general, however, there is a series of commonly-experienced stages in the mourning process.

These are:

- **Shock:** Numbness and disbelief are the usual first responses – often expressed in words like: 'No, I don't believe it', 'This can't be happening', or 'It doesn't make sense'. The bereaved person may seem stunned, confused, preoccupied, vague and incapable of taking much in.

   This can be disturbing for onlookers, who may even wonder whether the shock has affected the person's wits. However, this numbness actually serves quite a useful purpose; it is the mind's way of protecting itself from too much bad news all at once. A person in shock is in a highly vulnerable state and should be protected – but not overprotected.

Major decisions should be postponed if possible, but if decisions simply have to be made – such as those concerning funeral arrangements – the bereaved person should be involved, if only to have his or her opinions solicited. (More about who should share involvement in funeral arrangements in Chapter 6.)

- **Denial:** The bereaved person refuses to accept the loss, and carries on as though nothing is happening. This may seem a perverse refusal to face the facts, but is another form of adjustment to an overwhelming reality. In the case of job loss, the person may behave as though still employed, and even dress for work and leave home at the same time as before. In the case of serious illness, the individual may simply reject information or advice about his limitations, and may continue smoking or drinking or other behaviour he or she has been warned against. In the case of death of a loved one, denial may take the form of frequently 'seeing' him or her in a crowd, or 'sensing' him or her trying to communicate something. Such experiences, and the whole denial process, decline with time.

- **Anger and other intense emotions:** After the initial numbness wears off, the mourner experiences overwhelming emotions – grief, rage, regret at things done or undone, fear and anxiety, helplessness, restlessness and longing for what is lost. These feelings may swing wildly, and may even seem quite inappropriate, such as intense anger with the deceased.

Such feelings are not as irrational as they may seem; it's quite natural to feel angry at being left to cope with four children and a mortgage when the family breadwinner dies, for example. Anger may be displaced towards others, such as doctors for not doing enough to save the deceased.

Other apparently inappropriate emotions can include euphoria, or even a sudden 'deadening' of feeling. These don't mean that you are callous or uncaring, but are a form of 'time out' – the mind's way of giving itself a break from exhausting emotions.

- **Bargaining:** Another stage in coming to terms with the finality of loss, this stage is often expressed in 'If onlies' – 'If only I had called the doctor sooner, he/she wouldn't have died'; 'If I had only forbidden the use of the car, he/she wouldn't have had the accident', and so on. This is a common phase in people who are aware they are dying, who are in effect mourning their own deaths in advance. Their thoughts may go along the lines of 'If I eat only healthy food, I will get better', or even 'God, if only you let me beat this cancer, I promise to be a good person from now on'.

- **Depression:** A steady, sad hopelessness sets in after the first wild emotional storms have passed. The bereaved person feels apathetic and tired, and may become withdrawn and unable to take an interest in anything. This is a normal reaction to loss; but if it extends for too long or seems to be becoming chronic, professional advice should be sought.

- **Acceptance:** Eventually, in almost every case, the person will come to terms with his loss, and learn to live with it (or, in the case of facing one's own death, accept its inevitability and get on with the business of living in what time remains). There is a lot of truth in certain cliches, such as 'Time is a great healer' or the rather beautiful Biblical saying: 'Weeping can endure for a night, but joy comes in the morning'. The grieving process is unlikely to be completed so quickly, but weeping is an essential part of working through loss – and some joy almost certainly will eventually return to the bereaved person's existence. It will take time, however; every individual must work through grief at his own pace.

These stages are not necessarily experienced in this or any particular order. They may be felt more or less intensely, depending on the nature of the loss. Some people may pass through one or all of them faster, or may become 'stuck' at a particular phase, sometimes for years. How people cope with grief can be affected by all manner of factors, including:

- **How well prepared they were for the news:** It is easier to adjust to loss, however serious, if you have had time to prepare for it. That is why survivors of someone who dies unexpectedly – such as in a traffic accident – tend to have greater difficulty coping than survivors of someone who succumbed to a long illness.

- **The relationship with the deceased:** If this was troubled, the bereaved person may experience more difficulty sorting out his or her feelings and resolving the grieving process than someone with a happier or less complex relationship.

- **Accompanying changes:** A sense of loss is compounded if it involves other major life changes – such as moving house, reduced finances, commencing employment and so on.

- **The individual's health and state of mind:** A positive, robust individual is likely to be more resilient than an ill or unhappy person, though this is not invariably the case. Factors such as the individual's own sense of security – how he sees himself, his place in the family and the world – affect how he resolves grief. General psychological wellbeing also plays a part: grief can trigger or worsen any predisposition to mental illness. However, loss can be a great leveller, and it may be surprising who goes to pieces and who rises to the occasion.

- **Access to a support network:** The presence of loving friends and relatives, particularly those able to allow the bereaved person to vent his or her feelings, is a crucial factor in the resolution of grief. Ideally, such supporters should be able to listen without judgement or interruption, and should not belittle apparently silly or excessive emotions, such as guilt or self-blame for the loved one's death.

    The bereaved need to express such emotions in order to work through them.
    They should be permitted to cry or reminisce about the loved one, not told to 'buck up' or to 'pull yourself together' or other well meaning but essentially counterproductive advice. They certainly don't want to be told to 'look on the bright side' or that it's 'all for the best' (even if it is).

    Helping people through the mourning process can be stressful and harrowing, and not everybody is capable of it. Many people find death so disturbing that they avoid bereaved people at the time they most need support. It is not uncommon for neighbours and friends literally to cross the road to avoid them. This is deeply hurtful and only increases the mourner's sense of isolation. The neglectful friends are not being intentionally cruel, but are simply frightened of their own feelings – that they themselves may cry or break down.

It's not only friends who may be unable to offer support. If the family is one in which emotional displays are discouraged – where old-fashioned but ultimately self-destructive virtues prevail, such as 'being a man', and 'not making a fuss' – individuals can become locked into their own grief.

If a support network is unavailable or inadequate to the task at hand, professional bereavement counselling should be considered. For more about counselling, see Chapter 5.

HOW LONG WILL IT GO ON HURTING?

Mourners often want to know when they will 'feel better'. There is no sure answer to this question as the grief process is a very individual thing, as we've seen. Studies have shown that mourners who receive support and counselling seem to recover more quickly than those who don't, but working through grief is still a lengthy process which can't be hurried along.

The first 13 months is the acute phase; feelings of numbness and denial may persist for a month or more, gradually giving way to a sense of sorrow. Mourners may experience anxiety, withdrawal, irritability, aimlessness and preoccupation with thoughts of the deceased. Feelings of bitterness and guilt about not having done enough for him or her are also common. The anniversary of the death occurs within this period, which frequently causes a recurrence of painful and upsetting memories.

CASE HISTORY

'I learned who my real friends were when my husband died. Some of my best friends couldn't seem to face me when I was newly bereaved, and it's left a shadow over our subsequent relationship. They couldn't stand the intensity of my grief, I suppose, but it cut to the quick to find the invitations suddenly stopping – as though I'd died as well as Harry. Other people, and it was surprising whom some of them turned out to be, were more resilient. They let me cry and talk about him, which is something I still like to do. I love talking to people who knew Harry, particularly when he was young and at his best. It makes me feel as though he's not completely gone as long as someone remembers him. I feel very close to those people who were kind to me after the funeral and in the first few weeks and months.'

Beth, 67, retired

Most people begin to have an awareness of healing in the second year, though it can take two to five years to rebuild their lives around their 'grief life'. But there are no hard and fast time limits – often quite suddenly. You are on the way to recovery when you can think of the deceased without crying; simply enjoying remembering him or her and recalling positive moments in your relationship. Grief is a little like losing an arm – you're never 100 per cent again, but you can learn to work around it and eventually enjoy life again.

Chapter 3
The Toll Taken by Grief

It isn't only our emotions which take a beating during bereavement – our bodies don't take too kindly to it, either. In the *Mortality of Bereavement*, a study published in the *British Medical Journal*, researchers noted that the risk of dying within the first 12 months of bereavement was five times greater than for a control group. Informal studies of patients in palliative care units indicate that many suffered recent major losses, indicating a possible link with their present terminal illness. The old idea of dying of a broken heart is not so far off the mark; these are people who are basically pining.

STRESS AND DISEASE

Bereavement is a major cause of stress (see table on page 19). Stress suppresses the immune system, making us more susceptible to infection and disease. Some cancers, heart attacks, even adult onset diabetes may be triggered (not caused, for there will probably be an existing predisposition) by unresolved grief. Less dramatic but non-the-less real physical effects can include digestive problems, exhaustion (grieving is hard work), disturbed sleep and loss of appetite. These should become restored to normal after the shock of bereavement has abated. If they do not, it could be a sign of clinical depression.

Some mourners even experience symptoms of mimicking the deceased's illness, such as 'pseudo-angina' (chest pains with no physical cause) if the relative died of a heart attack.

DEPRESSION

Depression, as we've seen in the previous chapter, is a normal part of grief. It can take the form of frequent bouts of tears, feelings of

CASE HISTORY

'Several times in the weeks after my sister died, I had a real sense of her, that her spirit was trying to reach me and console me, to reassure me that everything was all right. That was a great comfort, even though I don't believe in the afterlife and I have no specific explanation for that feeling. It was probably only wish fulfilment, but it felt very real. I still have it occasionally.'

Melanie, 28, office manager

'deadness', hopelessness and withdrawal. Lack of energy and self-neglect are other symptoms of depression, and even cleaning the house or cooking for oneself may seem insurmountable tasks. If such depression becomes protracted, is accompanied by a change of character and/or doesn't respond to kind words or sympathetic attention, professional attention should be sought. Depression may be treated with counselling and drug therapy.

LOSS OF IDENTITY

Our perception of ourselves is often wrapped up in our relationships, and if we lose someone significant to us, we may also feel as though we have lost part of our own identity. For instance, a woman whose husband has died doesn't just lose her partner but her whole self-definition as 'wife'. Such as identity loss can involve a painful readjustment process and it may be months before she can begin to describe her new state as 'widow'.

LOSS OF SELF-ESTEEM

It is not uncommon for people suffering certain types of bereavement – such as parents of a disabled or stillborn child – to experience an acute sense of failure. They may put themselves down with statements like: 'I'm useless –

I can't even produce a healthy baby'. Disability or infertility can produce similar loss of self-esteem, as can marriage breakdown.

DIFFERING REACTIONS

Everyone who has suffered a bereavement (and that's pretty much the entire population, at some point in time) doesn't automatically sicken or die, of course, nor does their sense of identity or self-esteem necessarily plummet.

Even members of the same family who have experienced an identical loss do not react the same way; some may pine, others emerge relatively unscathed. The difference is how each individual relates to the loss, and whether he or she is able to express grief.

If not, this adds an additional strain to the stress of the loss itself, and this extra stress could be the straw that breaks the back of their resistance.

NORMAL OR ABNORMAL?

Some people, unused to the intensity of their emotions during the bereavement process, often wonder whether their reaction is excessive. They may be reassured by the fact that all the reactions listed in the four categories below are considered normal grief responses.

Normal grief reactions

Emotional:
- Anxiety
- Fear
- Sadness
- Anger
- Guilt
- Inadequacy
- Hurt
- Relief
- Loneliness

Physical:
- Hollowness in the stomach
- Tightness in the chest
- Tightness in the throat
- Over-sensitivity to noise
- A sense of depersonalisation
- Breathlessness
- Muscle weakness
- Lack of energy
- Dry mouth

Mental:
- Disbelief
- Confusion
- Preoccupation
- Sense of the dead person's presence
- Hallucinations

Behavioural:
- Crying
- Sleep disturbance
- Sighing
- Restlessness and over-activity
- Appetite disturbances
- Absentmindedness
- Social withdrawal
- Dreams of the deceased
- Avoiding reminders of the deceased
- Searching and calling out for the deceased
- Visiting places and carrying reminders of the deceased, or treasured objects which belonged to him or her.

(These reactions are based on the work of J. William Worden)

An abnormal grief reaction is one in which the survivor is unable to progress through the stages of grief but becomes stuck at a particular phase, such as denial, possibly for years.

This could be expressed in behaviour such as making a 'shrine' to the deceased – clothes or bedroom may be meticulously maintained, as though awaiting his or her return. Such survivors could benefit from bereavement counselling.

MEASURING STRESS

The Holmes-Rahe Survey of Recent Experiences – sometimes called the Social Readjustment Rating Scale (SRRS) – is a pioneering system of measuring stress devised by psychologists Holmes and Rahe in 1967. It is used as an indicator of the stress caused by traumatic life events, based on the degree of disruption they cause to the lifestyle and regular routine of the individual concerned. Typically stressful events, such as those mentioned in the table below, are assigned an arbitrary numerical value, measured in 'Life Change Units' (LCUs), that reflects their relative impact. The theory goes that the stress induced by such events can not only seriously affect the individual's health, it can also be cumulative. That means that a person who has just been divorced, for example, and whose living conditions have also changed (events scoring 73+25 LCUs respectively) is seen as suffering an equivalent amount of stress as someone whose spouse has died – which, at 100 LCUs, is seen as the greatest stressor of all. Someone suffering several stressful events in rapid succession – such as being separated, getting fired and incurring financial difficulties – would be seen at a commensurately greater risk of stress-related illness.

A 'recent' event need not be measured in time so much as whether you think it is still affecting you.

Table of Holmes-Rahe Stress Ratings

Life events	Life Change Units (LCUs)
Death of a spouse*	100
Divorce	73
Marital separation	65
Death of close family member	63
Personal injury or illness	53
Marriage	50
Fired at work	47
Retirement	45
Change in health of family member	44
Pregnancy	40
Sexual difficulties	39
Change in financial state	38
Death of close friend	37
Change to different line of work	36
Change in living conditions	25
Trouble with boss	23
Change in residence	20

*Death of a child is not included on this survey, but bereavement counsellors believe it would be rated close to the top of the chart.

Chapter 4
Death and Dying

We will all inevitably encounter death at some point, whether that of our parents, older relatives, friends, siblings or even our children. But because we've grown used to medical technology fixing all illnesses, we're not as familiar with its uncompromising face as our ancestors were.

Even as recently as the turn of the century, it was common for an individual to lose several children, even spouses, throughout his or her lifetime. The expression 'in the midst of life we are in death' held an all-too-literal truth.

People were more likely to die at home than in hospital, and the body remained in the home until it was buried. Under such circumstances, even quite small children came to have an understanding of death, unlike modern western society in which it is not uncommon to go throughout life without ever seeing or touching a dead person. It is often said that death has replaced sex as the last great taboo of modern life.

Over the last 20 years or so, however, death

has started to come out of the closet. This is largely due to the writings of Elisabeth Kubler-Ross, whose pioneering studies of the dying inspired and revolutionised bereavement care. The media has also helped to reacquaint us with death (at a distance) through graphic news coverage of wars, murders and accidents. Even so, our hands-on experience is probably fairly minimal until the moment (often in middle age or older) when our parents die. The terrible event that always happened to 'someone else' has finally happened to you – and you may not be at all sure how to deal with it.

There are four major categories of death, and each can have its own quite distinctive impact on survivors. They are:

- Natural death (from disease, old age)
- Accidental death
- Suicide
- Murder

Each of these can provoke a different intensity of grief, depending on how 'normal' they are perceived to be. For example, death of a parent after a long, full life may cause a great sense of loss and regret, but it does not seem as contrary to the natural order as the sudden death of a young child, who would not normally be expected to predecease his parents. Violent death is harder to come to terms with than, say, that of a 95-year-old who dies quietly in his sleep.

NATURAL DEATH

Grief will be influenced by how difficult, protracted or painful the death was, and how the dying person reacted to it; a harrowing death leaves lasting scars on the survivors. The state of the relationship with the person around the time of dying is another important factor. Many people reproach themselves for years if they failed to patch up differences, or weren't present at the actual moment of death.

Death of a parent can trigger a host of conflicting emotions. It is often the first real experience of the finality of death, as we've seen, which forces people to confront their own mortality. Many feel they have lost the only person who unconditionally loved and understood them, but along with the grief can come a sense of release or maturity. 'At last I feel grown up and in charge of my life' is a common sentiment.

Because we expect our parents to predecease us, we may have subconsciously begun the process of detachment a long time before the actual moment of death. For this reason, death of a parent usually affects adults less intensely than it does children, but the strength of familial bonds should not be underestimated, and many adults are profoundly moved and shaken by this event. On average, however, they are likely to be more strongly affected by the death of a spouse, the life partner with whom they expected to grow old. The death of siblings and close friends, whom they also expected to live as long as themselves, can be quite traumatic. Worst of all, however, in terms of loss for the future, is likely to be the death of a child (see page 25).

SUDDEN DEATH

Sudden death – such as from a traffic accident – is usually harder to accept than death following a long illness. A lingering death is very physically depleting for the relatives, but this can mean that they're exhausted enough to be able to let go when death finally comes. There's likely to be more unfinished business if someone's alive and well one minute then dead the next, because there has been no time to prepare and no time for goodbyes.

VIOLENT DEATH

Death by murder bequeaths a special torment to survivors. It can include the horror of dealing with police and having to attend inquests and trials, possibly years later, which stirs up all the old pain. But their grief is just as likely to be unresolved if the killer is not appre-hended, partly because of the fear that he might return. The trauma may be increased by intrusive media interest, sometimes years after the event, for example, on anniversaries of the crime.

CASE HISTORY

'This sounds a bit odd, and it's very difficult to explain, but after my son Evan died, I came up against what I call the Big Mystery. One minute he was there, the next he was gone. Where was he gone? How could the life force just evaporate like that? I kept thinking about it and thinking about it, and sometimes I felt I was coming close to some form of under-standing of what we're doing here and where we are going. But gradually all the petty details of everyday life took over and it slipped away. I feel a sense of failure here – I had an opportunity to understand something fundamental and important, and I let it go.'

John, 48, engineer

SUICIDE

Sometimes suicide may seem a reasoned, if not necessarily justified, response to a genuinely unbearable situation. For instance, someone facing a painful death from a terminal disease may prefer to choose their own way of dying.

It is more often a response to intense unhap-piness, undertaken, as the polite euphemism goes, when 'the balance of the mind is disturbed' – which is one way of saying that the idea of voluntarily cutting short one's life is so alien to most of us that we have to view it as madness.

Of all the forms of death, suicide is probably the hardest for the survivors to come to terms with. All of the usual grief reactions can become exaggerated and magnified. Suicide tends to be sudden and unexpected, which increases the shock and stress of grief, and this is deepened by the realisation that the person was so unhappy he or she actually sought death. This is such an inexplicable attitude to most of us that survivors may experience intense anger at the person who committed suicide. They may also become consumed with guilt, particularly if he or she left a bitter letter or the death was preceded by a quarrel. Feelings of having overlooked warning signs or even threats of suicide exacerbate this guilt. A sense of failure and rejection is also common.

WHEN A CHILD DIES

There is a lot of truth in the old saying: 'Lose your parent and you've lost your past; lose your spouse and you've lost your present; lose you child and you've lost your future'. Children are supposed to grow up and get old, not die before their lives have properly begun. The parents have not only lost a beloved child, they have also lost their trust in the world and the natural order of things. As well as terrible grief, this event leaves many parents with a feeling that they have failed as parents. They should be allowed to express this sense of failure; remarks like 'You mustn't blame yourself' or 'It's nobody's fault' simply don't connect with that parent's feelings.

Guilt is common when there is no obvious cause of death, as with cot death, or Sudden Infant Death Syndrome, in which babies up to the age of two simply stop breathing without warning. These deaths take place at home, not in hospital, and the parents are quite unprepared. Their shock is profound, and their need for reassurance great. Guilt feelings are compounded by the fact that the baby usually dies alone, out of the parents' sight, after being put to bed. If only, the parents think, they had checked the child earlier, spotted a warning sign or done something differently, the baby might still be alive.

Or blame may be displaced on to others, such as health professionals, who they feel should have picked up the problem sooner. Parental anguish is only increased by medical inquiries into the cause of death and other formalities. They need urgent support; help may be obtained from the Foundation for the Study of Infant Death (or get in touch with NABS – the National Association of

Bereavement Services – see page 98).

The grief can be different (if no less intense) when the child is older. We may be totally engrossed in a baby, instinctively responding to its helplessness with overwhelming love and protectiveness. But the parental relationship evolves and becomes more complex as the child grows, learns to talk and develops his or her own independent personality. Your child becomes more of a companion, even an equal, as he or she becomes older, particularly after adulthood, and a more complex relationship can elicit a more complex grief reaction, particularly if there had been conflict with the child, as is common during the rebellious teenage years. If the death was sudden, unexpected or accidental, there is all the shock and upsetting of normal expectations described above. If it is a result of illness, it is also a reversal of normal expectation (children are supposed to be brimming with health and vitality, not sick). Parental guilt can arise again; as spouses may blame themselves or one another for genetic weaknesses or family predispositions to diseases like cancer.

The death of a child places enormous strain on the parents' relationship, and the divorce rate following such bereavement is twice the national average for marital breakdown. Parents can be so shocked and stressed that they retreat into themselves, and may even unconsciously withdraw their love from their other children, fearful of reliving the agony should another child die.

Siblings of the deceased child may also withdraw, traumatised by the experience and/or their parents' reaction, or they may become clingy and nervous. Or they may become resentful, which may be expressed in outbursts of bad behaviour; or they may even feel responsible (if only they hadn't been naughty or unkind to the deceased child, this wouldn't have happened). The people upon whom they rely to help them now – their parents – can be so preoccupied with their own grief that they are unable to deal with their children's. Other loved family members – aunts, grandparents – may be similarly stricken, effectively leaving each family member alone with his or her grief.

Part of their stress comes from unrealistic social expectations; families are supposed to stick together and comfort one another during bereavement, but they can also heighten each other's distress. It may be better that mourners seek help outside the family circle. If they can let off steam – such as unexpressed feelings of blame towards a spouse for a child's death – to an 'outsider' (a trusted friend or counsellor), it can help exorcise the silent resentment corroding the relationship. Finding support outside the family allows you to come back to it refreshed and restored, drained of some of the bitterness and destructive energy of your feelings.

This may be obtained from friends, or through professional counselling. The isolation of grief may also be overcome with peer support from groups like Compassionate Friends, an association of bereaved parents (see page 99).

All these terrible emotions can be compounded by the fact that the death may have followed a deteriorating relationship or period of intense mutual unhappiness. It can be an additional nightmare if the survivor is called upon to identify the body, or answer police questions about the death. We've moved on from the days when suicides were excluded from Christian burial, but there is still a great stigma surrounding this type of death, which again only makes life harder for survivors.

There are no easy answers in this situation. All the advice given in Chapter 5 is particularly applicable to the survivors of those who died by murder and suicide, and they should take extra special care of themselves given their additional trauma. Peer support from the suicide survivors group may be helpful. For referral to such a group near you, contact the National Association of Bereavement Services (for contacts, see Helpful Addresses, page 98).

COMPOUND GRIEF

Compound or cumulative grief occurs when death follows death, as in war situations, or as with toll taken by AIDS on the gay community. Survivors never get a chance to recover before a new grief strikes, and can become physically numb and shell-shocked. Very old people, who have perhaps taken to reading the obituary columns to see which friends have died, may experience it. It is common among emergency workers and nursing staff in palliative care units (units set up not to heal the living, but to care for the dying). Carers need nurturing, too, and they may be assisted by counselling, stress management, 'debriefing' and attention from colleagues. It is important that such people learn to recognise and come to terms with their own vulnerability, particularly if they have become 'burnt-out' (when death no longer affects them at all). Then it is time to take time out to reassess their feelings and attitude to death and dying.

FACING YOUR OWN DEATH

People who are aware that they are going to die can react in very different ways. The very old and those exhausted by a long terminal illness seem to be better equipped to accept the cessation of being (and suffering). Others 'rage,

rage against the dying of the light', as Welsh poet Dylan Thomas put it. Younger people, and previously healthy people who suddenly find themselves with a diagnosis of terminal illness, often react with denial.

This may take different forms. The patient may simply not ask any questions or appears indifferent to his condition. He may withdraw and seem very quiet and preoccupied: or could assume a bright and breezy manner, deflecting concern from family and carers. Even though the physician may have been very frank about the seriousness of the prognosis, the patient may behave as though he is oblivious to it.

Such denial can be disturbing for the family, but should be respected. The patient is almost certainly aware of what is happening; his behaviour is in fact a useful defence mechanism, just as it is for bereaved people working through the mourning process. And that, of course, is what a terminally ill person is – bereft. He is mourning the loss of his life in advance, and needs time to come to terms with it.

HOW MUCH SHOULD THE PATIENT BE TOLD?

This prompts the question of how much should a terminal patient be told about his condition. The bad old days of 'sparing' the patient by keeping him in the dark have passed, as it was realised that most people, including young children, soon work out what is happening, if only from the family's behaviour. Being given inadequate or misleading information only increases their anxiety. As a general commonsense rule, all the patient's questions should be answered frankly and directly, but information probably shouldn't be forced on anyone who appears unready or uninterested in it. Many people will want to know how long they may expect to live; it would be unlikely (or unwise) for doctors to give a hard and fast figure, as both patient and family may become quite disturbed if they base their arrangements on a nominated time span which turns out to be incorrect. This can leave people who have worked their way through the process of detachment in a state of limbo.

'WHY ME?'

As well as denial, all the other stages of the grieving process may also come into play, and the dying person may react with anger 'Why is this happening to me? What did I do to deserve this?' – particularly if he is experiencing pain and other distressing symptoms. Fear – of more pain; of desertion and separation from loved ones; of losing control, becoming incompetent and a burden on others; worries about financial arrangements and the family's future welfare; sorrow at not having accomplished enough during life and fear of dying – can also affect his behaviour. He may become regressive and childish, querulous, demanding and plain unpleasant to deal with. Over time, he may lapse into depression and finally achieve a degree of acceptance of the situation.

Many of these reactions can be difficult for carers to endure, but it is important that they realise that most dying people have a great need for the unconditional love and support of family and friends. Just as other bereaved people, they may feel a great desire to talk, to put their life in perspective. Simply being available to listen, in an unhurried, non-judgmental way, can be a great solace. Many people are afraid of or confused by death. This may be expressed by avoiding or being unnatural with a dying person, contributing to feelings of loneliness and isolation. These may be allayed by sitting quietly with such a person, allowing him to be silent or speak as he wishes.

The family and friends of the dying person are also under considerable strain, and need as much support as possible. They also may be helped by the advice in Chapter 5.

COMING TO TERMS WITH DEATH AND DYING

One reason why the bereavement process is so painful is that, as we've seen, it forces us to confront our own mortality. How we react is to a degree dependent upon our beliefs about what happens after death – is it the end of being, or is there any sort of existence in the hereafter? If there is, what form might it take, and could it include the possibility of being reunited with loved ones?

If you haven't worked out your own attitudes to these questions, you're going to have a harder time coming to terms with death, whether of others or more particularly of your own life drawing to a close. If so, you may benefit from asking yourself exactly how you view death and how it differs from life; what you think you will be and how you will feel when you die; and what, if anything, would help you overcome your fear of death. Be as honest with yourself as possible; your answers may surprise you.

Chapter 5
Things That Can Help

Nothing can 'fix' your grief. You can't bring the dead back to life (or restore what has gone, in the case of other kinds of loss). You may find it hard to believe now, in the first shock of bereavement, but there are a number of things you and others can do to help you work through your grief. Some of them, such as the first two or three points below, may seem very painful at the time, but will help expedite the healing process and ultimately make you feel better.

VIEWING THE BODY

Seeing and even touching the body before burial helps you acknowledge the reality of death. It confers a finality upon the event, underlying that there is a beginning and an end to life. Ask the funeral director or hospital staff to arrange a viewing. Even if the body has been mutilated in a traffic accident, you can still uncover the hand, say. Just touching a finger would help the survivor to acknowledge the finality of death and begin the process of understanding.

THE IMPORTANCE OF THE FUNERAL

Well-meaning friends sometimes attempt to spare bereaved people pain by taking over the funeral arrangements and organising everything for them. But this in effect excludes them from one of life's most important rites of passage.

They should be involved as much as possible in the arrangements, to allow them a symbolic way of saying goodbye. For the same reason, it's important that all those affected by the death (even small children) attend the funeral. More about arranging a funeral in the following chapter.

UNFINISHED BUSINESS

With any sudden death – accidental or otherwise – there is likely to be considerable 'unfinished business' and survivors may find themselves unable to let go, even after some time has passed. It's important that they be encouraged to work through such business. This could be accomplished by writing a letter expressing all the things that they would have liked to have had an opportunity to express to the deceased – sorrow, love or regret for not having done enough for them, even anger at having been left in a bad financial position, everything that seems important. This letter could be symbolically 'posted' to the deceased, perhaps by burying it near the grave, or at the site where death occurred, or indeed any place which seems significant to the survivor (even a 'happy' one, such as where they first met). Another way of completing such unfinished business is to vocalise these feelings – say out loud everything you feel, as though addressing the dead person. Even if you find yourself shouting what seem to be terrible things – such as blaming the deceased for contributing to his own death – this process can give an enormous sense of release.

SHOW YOUR GRIEF

While the wearing of mourning garb is increasingly uncommon in our society, it is important to make some sort of symbolic statement of how you hurt. Some bereavement experts believe that it is far healthier to react the way certain non-western societies do; in the traditional Aboriginal response to death, for example, the body would be on view for three days, during which time the women would wail until their emotions were exhausted. The men would cut themselves with 'worry cuts' to demonstrate the pain they were feeling inside.

An equivalent gesture today could be simply wearing a black arm band.

EXPRESS YOUR FEELINGS

When a loved one dies, survivors usually want to talk about the dead person, mulling over their memories and putting their relative's life in perspective. A sympathetic ear and a willingness to listen is of real assistance now. It also helps mourners to be allowed to express their hurt and all the other bad feelings. Men, who are traditionally taught to contain their emotions, are more likely to react angrily than women, who seem more able to express feelings of sorrow and confusion.

Supporters tend to withdraw from anger, but it's important that they realise that all mourners need support, whatever course their grieving takes.

Unfortunately, the very intensity of these feelings may cause friends to become uncomfortable and try to change the subject. They may even accuse the bereaved person of being 'morbid'; but a preoccupation with a lost loved one is not morbid, it's an integral, essential and healthy part of the mourning process. If friends or family are unequal to the task (and they are often mourning the same loss themselves, and incapable of giving much support) professional bereavement counselling can help.

CASE HISTORY

'My father died five years ago and I still haven't got over it. I don't know if I ever will. He died of a heart attack, very suddenly — it was the classic "drop dead" scenario. But even though he seemed to be fine just before his death, when we went through his things later we found bottle after bottle of tablets for angina (chest pain). He'd been in bad pain the whole time, and we hadn't noticed. That made me feel terrible. But at the same time I felt furious with him, for how were we supposed to know how he felt if he kept putting on a big act all the time?

'My first emotion was overwhelming guilt — I wondered if he knew how much I'd loved him, and wished I'd made it plainer when he was alive. Our last couple of years had been a bit tense, mostly because of his money problems and the way he abused his health. I think my main emotion now is anger.

'Anger about the way he didn't take care of himself, and anger that he just pegged out like that, leaving me to cope with the financial mess he'd made. I still cry when I'm alone, but I never cried in public, not even at the funeral. They say you should get it off your chest, talk it out, but who to? There's a limit to what you can burden your friends with. So who?'

Colin, 34, landscaper

PROFESSIONAL HELP

Bereavement counsellors are trained to identify the stages of the grieving process, to
'permit' tears and other expressions of loss, to
help develop coping strategies, and generally
assist and expedite the grief work.

They will encourage mourners to view the
body and may even accompany them, and may
also offer support around the anniversary of
the death, when feelings of grief often resur-
face. The best time for seeking assistance is
usually about six weeks after the funeral,
when people tend to stop rallying around and
leave you on your own to cope. This is the time
at which mourners are usually at their most
vulnerable, as the denial stage ends and grim
reality sinks in.

For referral to a support group and/or grief
counsellor, contact the National Association of
Bereavement Services (see page 98). There
may be a free counselling service in your area –
ask your doctor what is available, or check
your local telephone directory. Hospital social
workers may be able to refer people suffering
loss of a loved one, or reaction to illness or
disability, to the appropriate services; so may
social workers within the coronial system.

There are also telephone counselling services
run by groups such as the Samaritans (see page
101).

SURVIVORS' GROUPS

One of the worst things you can say to a bereft person is :'I know exactly how you feel'. This may be well-meant, but can have the effect of invalidating that person's unique experience of grief. You may imagine how he or she might feel, but nobody can truly enter into the feelings of another human being. However, bereft people can derive considerable consolidation from others who have undergone similar bereavements – simply seeing that they have survived the now seemingly unendurable can help. Peer support is available from groups such as Cruse for widows and widowers, SANDS (Stillbirth And Neo-natal Death Society), Compassionate Friends (for bereaved parents), the Foundation for the Study of Infant Death, suicide support groups and so on. See pages 98–101 for support groups covering different types of bereavement.

AVOID UNNECESSARY CHANGE

Change – any sort of change – causes stress, and the last thing needed now is additional sorrow. Survivors often try to get away from their grief by selling up and starting afresh somewhere else; but they simply end up burdening themselves with the extra strain of adjusting to a new life. Well-meaning children may pressure Mum or Dad into living with them after the death of a spouse; but all this means is that he or she loses a home and familiar surroundings as well as a partner. Widowers often remarry soon after the death of their wives, because they cannot bear their new lone status (widows tend to be more cautious); but they could be marrying for the wrong reasons and such 'rebound' unions can develop problems. Don't make important decisions in a crisis atmosphere; give yourself time to think through what you really want and need. Even people facing retirement – which involves coming to terms with the ending of their careers – are advised not to sell their homes or move away for at least a year, to allow a considered appraisal of their new needs.

DIET

It's particularly important to pay attention to nutrition, to resist stress-induced illness, but this is a need which many bereaved people, depressed and lacking in appetite, find easy to let slip. A common response to the bereaved is to offer food for comfort – a neighbour may pop around with a casserole, friends issue dinner invitations – and this should be accepted without embarrassment; you need looking after now.

DROWNING YOUR SORROWS

It's important not to blot out reality with alcohol or tranquillisers, even though friends and even doctors may attempt to ply you with one or the other to calm you down. Such chemical numbing doesn't cure but only postpones grief; it simply puts off the evil day of having to accept loss.

EXERCISE AND RELAXATION

The enormous stress of bereavement, and accompanying physical problems, may be lessened by a program of relaxation. This can involve undertaking specific stress-reduction activities such as yoga, tai chi, massage or meditation. Regular moderate exercise has a host of health benefits, including relieving anxiety and countering depression. Make a point of taking a brisk walk, playing a game of tennis or swimming a few pool lengths whenever possible; it will help cheer you and get you out of yourself.

AT WORK

Some try to bury their grief in work (this can take somewhat extreme forms, such as going straight from the funeral back to the office).

However, you're unlikely to be performing at your best for quite a while, as the stress of bereavement typically affects your powers of judgement and concentration. Avoid major projects and critical decisions, and try to delegate as much as practicable; you should expect from your colleagues at least as much as you expect from yourself.

There are many types of work, not just the paid sort you do in an office. It is not uncommon for newly widowed women, for example, to throw themselves into looking after their children, neglecting their own needs. They may think: 'I'm all they've got now, I must try to make up to them for the loss of their father.' But they are not doing the right thing by themselves or the children if they drive themselves to the point of breakdown. Perhaps they now need to go out to work for financial reasons, increasing the strain and demands on them. Again, this is not the time to be proud or demonstrate your independence; accept any help offered if normal household chores, child-minding and so on seem to be too much for you.

BE GENTLE WITH YOURSELF

The old-fashioned view of mourning, in which people retreated from the world for up to a year, treating themselves virtually as invalids, is not as far off the mark as it may seem. You have sustained a considerable shock to your system – physical and emotional – and it is important to rest and look after yourself as well as possible in those crucial first few weeks and months.

Pay attention to yourself – make yourself go on outings, even if you don't feel like it; comfort yourself as you would others with little treats or rewards. Simply taking the time to have your hair done can be a tonic. So can buying yourself a box of chocolates, reading a trashy novel or seeing an escapist film. If you normally have pretty high standards of what you expect from yourself, lower them now. Indulge yourself; this is no time for battling on or keeping a stiff upper lip.

Work through the checklist on page 46.

OTHER KINDS OF GRIEF

Some of the points above relate specifically to death of a loved one; most relate to all kinds of grief, whether from divorce, trauma, job loss or disability. More about these kinds of grief in the following chapters.

SELF-HELP CHECK LIST

- Express your grief.
- If you feel the need for support, consider professional bereavement counselling.
- View the body – it will help.
- Attend the funeral.
- Avoid major changes until the shock of grief has subsided.
- Attend to 'unfinished business' – maybe by writing a letter to the deceased.
- Look after yourself – try to eat, sleep and exercise properly, and avoid stress in the workplace as much as possible.

Chapter 6
Organising a Funeral

In our society, it can be quite common to spend up to a year planning a wedding, but many of us may only allocate an hour or two to a rite of passage at least as important: the funeral. But rushing this important and significant event can leave a residue of guilt, resentment and unresolved grief, particularly if you delegate the arrangements to the funeral director or friends, only to find them unsatisfactory after the event.

Most of us come quite unprepared to this task, never having thought of it before the moment of bereavement, when we are least able to make considered decisions. In order to organise the funeral of your choice, it helps to know beforehand exactly what happens when someone dies, and what options are available to survivors. This chapter is intended to dispel some of the mystery surrounding the funeral process.

MY RELATIVE HAS JUST DIED – NOW WHAT?

If someone dies at home, the first thing you would do is ring the family doctor, who would examine the body and issue a death certificate.

If he was not certain of the cause of death, he would notify the coroner. The coroner then notifies the police. The coroner will decide if a post mortem is necessary, and his officer will arrange for the body to be brought to the mortuary to establish the cause of death. The next of kin may have a medical representative present at the post mortem if they wish. After the post mortem the body will be released for the funeral.

This process, which usually takes a couple of days, doesn't mean that the death is necessarily suspicious, simply that its cause is not immediately obvious.

If the doctor does sign a death certificate, the next step is to contact a funeral director, who will remove the body to the funeral home pending the funeral, if desired. This is not obligatory, and some people may prefer to keep the body at home for viewing by relatives and friends. The funeral director then contacts the family to discuss the funeral arrangements.

WHO SHOULD ORGANISE THE FUNERAL?

Bereaved people may be so distressed that friends may try to 'spare' them pain by taking over all the decisions about services, coffins, flowers and so on. Such kindness may have the unintended effect of cheating them of the opportunity to mark an intensely significant event. They could be left feeling like outsiders at the funeral if they have contributed nothing to the arrangements, which will not help in the long term. Sympathetic friends could perhaps assist with a lot of the legwork (such as ascertaining the options and best service available), but allow the bereaved person the final say on the arrangements.

TAKE YOUR TIME

The most important thing is to remember that there is no hurry; you do not have to rush into arrangements or commitments the day the person dies. Some people feel they have to organise everything on the spot, but they should perhaps wait until other family members, who may want to make an input, arrive. Take a few days to work out exactly what you want, and then ask the funeral director to arrange it. You are under no obligation to accept any 'standard arrangements' which may be offered.

EXPLORE THE OPTIONS

● **Viewing the body:** As we've seen, viewing the body is a chance to say goodbye, to say the things that you may have left unsaid, or that society often won't let you say. Many funeral directors offer this opportunity; if not, ask for it. You may choose to dress the deceased in a favourite outfit (you can do this, or ask the funeral director to do it, or even do it together).

● **The coffin:** Bereaved people are often battling with unconscious guilt feelings which they may try to assuage by selecting lavish and expensive appointments. In such a vulnerable state it is easy to be influenced into costly decisions, so you should be aware that there is a great variety of coffins and caskets available. You do not have to accept the first offered.

● **The service:** You may prefer to have a church service, or a service conducted by secular celebrant. It doesn't have to be in a church or chapel; there is nothing to stop you having a memorial service (without the body) or the funeral service (with the body) anywhere you choose – on a boat, in a park or some place of sentimental significance. Nor does the service necessarily have to precede cremation or burial. You could, for instance, take the cremated ashes anywhere you choose to conduct a service of your choice (perhaps with a photograph of the deceased). The ashes don't have to remain at the crematorium, unless desired; you can take them to keep at home, bury them under a tree, scatter them over the ocean – whatever seems appropriate to you.

A CELEBRATION OF A LIFE

Remember that the funeral is not for the dead, it is for the living. The aim should be not to provide the deceased with arrangements that would not have gratified him or her, but to allow survivors to say a meaningful 'goodbye'.

Funerals don't have to be viewed as something terribly distressing to be got over as fast as possible, but should be a celebration, or at least commemoration of the deceased person. For this reason, it can be helpful to have several friends contribute with eulogies, anecdotes, even jokes, rather than to leave it all to a lone minister, who may not even have known the deceased.

Humour is not necessarily out of place at funerals; it doesn't have to be tremendously solemn and religious, unless this feels appropriate to you.

Favourite songs could be played; home movies of the deceased could be shown; cherished possessions could be displayed by the coffin or even placed in it (jewellery, toys, even a beer can, if that was part of the deceased person's persona!). It may be helpful if the funeral is tape-recorded or video-taped – it can often be therapeutic for family and friends to reflect on what was said and/or sung.

Don't be intimidated by custom or tradition; it is you, the bereaved person's day, and it is up to you how you run it.

THE LAW

Many people mistakenly believe that all sorts of regulations must restrict your choice of funeral arrangements and disposal of the body. This is not the case; you are under no obligation to use the services of a funeral director, for example, and there is nothing to stop you making your own coffin or conducting your own funeral if you wish. You can bury the body at sea (contact the Ministry of Agriculture, Food and Fisheries for details and regulations) or even in your garden (planning permission and the appropriate approval have to be sought from your local authority. Clearly it makes sense to give these ideas careful consideration, especially as you may not always be living in your present location.

YOUR RIGHTS

You are entitled to funeral arrangements that you are happy with, but it is not uncommon for bereaved people to feel hustled into unwanted decisions. It can avoid unhappiness if you make a point of meeting the funeral director you choose face to face (rather than negotiating over the phone), and inspecting his premises, or those of the crematorium and cemetery.

Ask whether the funeral director is a member of a reputable professional organisation (such as the National Association of Funeral Directors, see page 98).

If this appears unseemly, or you simply don't feel up to insisting on your rights, ask a sympathetic friend to do these things for you. Don't feel that it is disrespectful to the deceased to query the arrangements. Dissatisfaction with them may prove an enduring source of unhappiness and resentment, hindering the completion of the grieving process.

SELF-HELP CHECK LIST

- Involve yourself in the funeral arrangements.
- Don't rush things – take the time to get the arrangements the way you want them.
- Consider your options – there are many different ways to organise a funeral.
- Remember, a funeral is for the living, not the dead.
- Remember, also, that a funeral is a commemoration of a life – it can be joyful, or even funny, without necessarily showing disrespect to the deceased.

Chapter 7

Miscarriage and Stillbirth

An estimated 15 to 25 per cent of early preg-
nancies ends in miscarriage, so this is an experience that many women will face at some
point in their reproductive life. But despite all
the articles in women's magazines, miscarriage
is still a subject on which there is a conspiracy
of silence. Too many people still regard it as a
non-event; there are no rituals or rites to mark
the event, only trivialising remarks like 'You'll
soon have others'.

AN UNACKNOWLEDGED LOSS

Miscarriage causes a deep emotional reaction
in virtually all women, and many are quite
unprepared for the intensity of their feelings. It
really is a little death, only there's no cere-
mony, no body, no funeral, no sympathy
cards. There's nothing to show, so people may
behave as though nothing has happened.

For this reason, mourning over miscarriage
can fall into the category of 'disenfranchised'

grief discussed in Chapter 1.

Deep grief is expected and tolerated with the death of a full-term child. Yet miscarriage is often viewed in a very different light; as you were only 'a little bit pregnant', you should only be a little bit sad. But it's the feelings involved, not the length of the pregnancy, that are important. For many women, bonding begins pre-birth, and when their pregnancy ends abruptly or with very little warning, they experience acute sorrow and anxiety.

GUILT AND CONFUSION

Miscarriage often provokes feelings of guilt, which can take the form of seemingly bizarre self-reproach. Even if the pregnancy is planned, many women wonder: 'Am I ready to become a mother?' Then, when they miscarry, they think. 'Maybe my baby knew how I felt'. They tell themselves they're defective because they can't even produce a baby; or they blame the miscarriage on the fact that they kept on smoking or drinking, worked too hard, or had sex with their partners.

This guilt can find expression in the questions women who have miscarried almost invariably ask their doctors: 'Why did it happen? Was it something I did that I shouldn't have done? Or something that I didn't do that I should have done?'

Unhappily, they may never receive the

answer to these questions. While around 60 per cent of miscarriages are caused by chromosomal abnormalities in the foetus, the causes of the remaining 40 per cent are unknown. If the doctor or medical professional can't provide a specific reason for the miscarriage, it only adds to the woman's anxiety and confusion.

The burden of such negative emotions can be increased by the fact that many women undergoing curettage to remove the remaining 'products of conception', as the rather off-putting medical expression goes, are sometimes hospitalised alongside women who are having an abortion. Miscarrying women find it very painful to see live babies at this time. These feelings can linger for months, even years, and may deepen around the anniversaries of the expected birth date and date of the miscarriage.

THE FATHER'S FEELINGS

The father's grief may be even more 'disenfranchised' than the woman's. His emotional needs are often overlooked and many people fail to recognise that he too was a potential parent. This can be especially hard when the man is often the one who informs friends and relatives of the miscarriage. Men can feel a deep sense of loss at this time, but often try to keep their feelings under wraps to avoid upsetting their partners even further. This apparent passivity can be mistaken for indifference, by the partner as well as outsiders.

FAMILY PROBLEMS

Some parents shirk telling their children of the miscarriage for fear of distressing them. But this is counterproductive if the children were aware of the pregnancy; they're likely to be quite disturbed if the promised new brother or sister not only fails to materialise but is never mentioned again. They may be too young to understand truly what has been lost, but they can sense their parents' anxiety. It's important to give them simple, factual information about what has happened, and explain why Mummy and Daddy are feeling sad and need their loving support.

HELPING THE HEALING

Because miscarriage is such a taboo topic, many people have difficulty in understanding that women who have experienced it feel a great need to express their sense of loss. If the pregnancy was unannounced, these women may suffer in silence. If they have announced it, they have to endure the pain of revealing the sad news, only to find their loss is not properly acknowledged. They may even fail to acknowledge its full toll to themselves.

CASE HISTORY

'I miscarried my first pregnancy at 10 weeks and I was very, very upset; more upset than you'd expect, considering that I'd only known I was pregnant for about three weeks. What hurt most was the way my GP broke the news. She said: "Miscarriage is nature's way of getting rid of its mistakes – you wouldn't want to have a deformed baby, would you?"

'What an incredibly insensitive thing to say, particularly for another woman! She couldn't possibly have known whether the baby was deformed or not! I supposed she was trying to console me, but it only made me feel like some sort of freak, producing baby monsters. I never went back to that doctor again.'

Susan, 28, teacher

As with other forms of grief, women who have miscarried should not deny their grief, or try to keep it secret. They should allow themselves to mourn, and let others – family, friends – know how they feel.

It also helps to:

● Try to find out as much as you can about miscarriage in general, and your own experience in particular. The more medical information you have, the less likely you are to torture yourself with fruitless speculation and self-blame.

● Don't neglect your partner's feelings – remember, he has lost a child too.

See page 100 for a miscarriage support group contact address and telephone number.

STILLBIRTH AND DEATH OF A NEWBORN

This event has considerably more status than miscarriage, but may still go unaccompanied by some of the healing rites of passage of other forms of death. However important that child may be to its parents, it has no identity to anyone outside the family. It has never been seen or introduced to the wider community, so the parents' grief tends to be discounted and often unacknowledged.

It is not so long since stillborn children weren't even accorded the dignity of their own funeral but simply buried at the foot of other people's graves; whisked out of the mother's sight and disposed of, like something that was never meant to be.

As with the death of an older child, the parents have to contend with the weight of loss of the future life of their child. Birth is supposed to be an exciting, positive event, full of potential for the future.

If a woman goes into a maternity hospital only to emerge childless, she is not only shocked and bereft, but she may well be greeted by silence from nonplussed friends. They may avoid the subject for fear of

WHEN A CHILD GOES MISSING

Every year thousands of children leave home and simply disappear, as far as their parents are concerned. They may literally never see their children again, or at least not for many years, during which time the missing offspring are 'dead' to them. The parents' grief in such situations falls into the 'disenfranchised' category, as the world at large fails to acknowledge their feelings. As the child's departure is often the culmination of a long period of domestic tension and unresolved conflict – perhaps resulting from parental neglect or abuse, or from the child's resentment of a parent's remarriage or de facto relationship – the parents can be left with strong feelings of guilt. Their agony may be compounded by not knowing whether the child is alive or dead. This is often manifested in nightmares and 'searching' behaviour (constantly looking for the child, consciously or otherwise). The National Missing Persons Helpline offers practical advice and support to the families of those who are missing (see page 100).

upsetting the parents, but the most hurtful thing is to ignore their loss, as though the baby never existed.

It is now realised that it is important that the child's identity, individuality and existence be fully acknowledged.

For example, it should be given a name, as well as a funeral or at least some sort of commemorative ritual. It also helps if the parents are given an opportunity to spend time with the baby before burial, both to get to know it and to say goodbye.

Such things as holding and cuddling the child, and taking pictures for the family album, should not be seen as spooky or distasteful, but as beneficial in beginning the process of coming to terms with the loss.

Other family members, including children, should be allowed to participate in this. Seeing and touching a dead sibling will not damage a child, as long as he is properly prepared (and there is no gross abnormality in the baby); his imagination is more likely to run riot with frightening fantasies about death if he is excluded or kept in the dark. Abnormality should not be a reason for 'sparing' the mother and father sight of the baby, however; while it will be disturbing at the time, it may ultimately help reconcile them to the fact that death was inevitable, and perhaps the best thing for the child itself.

SELF-HELP CHECKLIST

- Acknowledge your grief, even if others don't. You have lost a child, and have every right to grieve.
- Try to view and touch the child if possible.
- Acknowledge the child's individuality and personhood. Give it a name and a funeral if possible and appropriate.
- Be aware that your partner and family are also grieving – don't expect too much from them.
- Find out as much as you can about still birth and miscarriage, to dispel the mystery that can add to your grief.

HOW TO HELP OTHERS

- If you know someone who has experienced miscarriage or stillbirth, allow her to talk about her feelings.
- Don't be silent – acknowledge her loss with a card or a sympathetic remark.
- Try to be especially sensitive around the time the child was to be born, or on the anniversary of the birth in the case of a stillbirth.
- Remember to include her partner and the rest of the family in your sympathy.

Chapter 8
Surviving Trauma

Life seems to have become a chancy business in recent years. Zeebrugge, King's Cross, Hungerford, Lockerbie, Hillsborough, Hagley School Mini-bus crash, together with hostage sieges, bank robberies – a never-ending list of disasters and terrible crimes erupts around us on an almost daily basis.

Simply reading about them in the newspaper leaves you with feeling that the world is a wild and threatening place. What effect does it have on the witnesses and survivors of the actual events – people who have seen others horribly injured or struck dead without warning; or have been hurt themselves by inexplicable and uncontrollable events; whose whole world has been turned upside down within a few seconds?

By and large, they experience shock and great distress. Such people are trauma victims – unwilling participants in terrible and catastrophic events – and they typically respond with an acute grief reaction (though this may go unrecognised by themselves and others at the time). For while they may not have lost anyone close to them, they have lost their perception of the world as a safe and predictable place. They experience an over-whelming sense of helplessness and powerless-ness, which can make them feel like victims. It can also induce what is called 'survivor guilt' (a feeling of having undeservedly escaped a terrible fate which engulfed others).

Post-traumatic stress syndrome is a normal reaction to abnormal circumstances. It was first documented in soldiers fighting the Vietnam war, but it's now recognised that it's not just wars, disasters and other headline-grabbing events that provoke it. More mundane but still disturbing events – such as seeing someone drop dead from a heart attack or being involved in a car accident – are also highly traumatic. Police, rescue workers and medical personnel, routinely confronted by suffering or death, are particularly susceptible to trauma.

SYMPTOMS OF TRAUMA

Trauma victims experience all the normal grief reactions, which can be exaggerated by the sudden shock of the experience in question, as well a by its legal aftermath (police ques-tioning, media interest, inquests and trials). In this respect their experience is similar to that of survivors of murder or sudden death.

Symptoms of a stress reaction to trauma include:

Physical:
- Nausea
- Upset stomach
- Tremors (lips, hands)
- Feeling uncoordinated
- Sweating
- Chills
- Diarrhoea
- Dizziness
- Chest pains
- Rapid heart beat
- Rapid breathing
- Increased blood pressure
- Headaches
- Muscle aches
- Sleep disturbances

(*NB:* All these can be signs of stress, but can also signal dangerous disorders and should be checked out by a doctor – particularly symptoms such as chest pains.)

Intellectual:
- Slowed thinking
- Difficulty making decisions and solving problems
- Confusion
- Disorientation (time and place)
- Memory problems
- Difficulty concentrating and calculating
- Difficulty naming objects
- 'Reliving' the event over and over again
- Distressing dreams
- Poor attention span

Emotional:
- Anxiety
- Fear
- Guilt
- Grief
- Depression
- Sadness
- Feeling lost, abandoned and isolated
- Worry about others
- Wanting to hide
- Wanting to limit contact with others
- Anger
- Irritability
- Numbness
- Feeling shocked or startled

If symptoms are severe or if they last longer than six weeks, the traumatised person may need counselling.

CASE HISTORY

A man had to go into hospital to have cancer surgery, so his wife and daughter postponed a planned holiday abroad in order to visit him in hospital. They were both murdered – innocent bystanders – in a shopping centre shootout the day before he was discharged. As well as his intense grief over the senseless and shocking event, the man had to contend with the feeling that he was in some way responsible for what had happened; if only they hadn't stayed behind to look after him, his wife and daughter would be alive today. Such 'survivor guilt' is typical of trauma victims.

PROFESSIONAL HELP

There has been considerable study and research into trauma in the past decade or so, with the development of trauma clinics and the like. Many major institutions have developed what are called 'critical incident management plans' to help them cope with the aftermath of any future crises. Stress and bereavement specialists often work with the emergency services, and move in quickly at disaster scenes to assist trauma victims.

It is now recognised that such victims can be helped, and the intensity of any post-traumatic stress reaction reduced, by two things:

● **Defusing:** Simply telling someone what has happened. This is not counselling, but an opportunity to ventilate their thoughts and feelings, to 'burst the bubble' of their shock and horror. Defusing, ideally conducted by a trained mental health worker, should take place on site as soon as possible (within 24 hours). Defusing is particularly useful for 'helpers' (rescue workers, casualty nurses and so on) to give them 'time out' from shocking events in their daily duties.

● **Debriefing:** A further opportunity to talk over what has happened, only now the trauma victim will be helped to explore his feelings and reactions to that event (then and now), asked about any symptoms of stress he may be experiencing, and given information on dealing with it. Debriefing, which is usually done on a group basis, should take place between 24 and 72 hours of the traumatic event, after there has been time to assimilate what has happened. Debriefing facilitators are mental health professionals who are trained to identify people 'at risk' – tearful, shaking, withdrawn – who may need extra help in coping.

Survivors' groups can help although they may eventually become counter-productive, fixating the person on the traumatic event and not allowing him or her to move on. If you feel you need help ask your doctor what is available locally. You may wish to contact Disaster Action, a charity whose members are all survivors or bereaved from disasters such as Lockerbie and Hillsborough, to talk to those with a similar experience (see page 100). Not every trauma victim will have the opportunity of formal defusing and debriefing, particularly those whose experience has been less obvious than that of survivors of some national disaster. But they may still be very distressed by witnessing an event such as, say, someone committing suicide by throwing himself under their local train.

Such 'unnoticed' trauma victims could consult the National Association of Bereavement Services (see page 98), or their doctor, for help.

SELF-HELP CHECKLIST

It is important that trauma victims realise that what they are experiencing is normal, not crazy; their feelings, while painful, are part of the healing process. There's not much you can do to avoid these uncomfortable feelings, but there are things that can erase the pain associated with a traumatic event:

- Within the first 24 hours, periods of strenuous exercise alternated with relaxation will help overcome some of the physical reaction. Thereafter, you should try to get adequate rest and maintain a well-balanced diet. Many of the suggestions in Chapter 5 may be useful to you now.
- Spend time with friends, and try to talk to people who love you.
- Structure your time; keep busy with your normal activities and routine, if you feel able.
- Consider keeping a journal to help 'write out' your feelings.
- Don't try to fight flashbacks or recurring thoughts and dreams of the event. These will decrease over time and become less painful.
- Share your feelings, particularly with people who experienced the same traumatic event and those helping them and you.
- Seek counselling if your feelings seem prolonged or unduly intense.

HOW TO HELP OTHERS

- Listen carefully.
- Spend time with the traumatised person.
- Reassure them that they are safe.
- Don't take their anger or other feelings personally.
- Be sensitive.
- Be patient and loving.

Chapter 9
Illness and Disability

'Cheer up – you're not dead yet.' That's a common saying, and one from which people who are ill or have become physically impaired may take some comfort. Or they may not. For disease and disability are also forms of loss – loss of perfect health, of a body which effortlessly obeyed their wishes – which provoke their own bereavement reaction.

Events such as loss of the ability to walk, mastectomy, loss of a limb, stroke or coronaries, chronic pain and diseases such as asthma and diabetes can all take a considerable toll on a person's identity and self-esteem.

Old skills may need to be relearned, virtually every aspect of life may have to be adapted to accommodate the disability, and a future which once seemed full of promise now offers limited options.

PROBLEMS, PROBLEMS

It's not just the physical impairment which has

to be adjusted to; there can be a host of accompanying emotional difficulties which take time and hard work to come to terms with. Sickness is a compelling intimation of mortality – if part of your heart muscle can die during a coronary, it is a reminder that so, ultimately, the whole organism will die.

Loss of previously taken-for-granted physical powers can be humiliating, particularly if it involves requiring assistance for such intimate functions as bathing, dressing and going to the toilet.

Fear of the future, of further attacks of a serious disease, if not death, can be very debilitating; as can worries about loss of income and becoming a burden on family and friends. A person who has been disfigured, or lost a limb, can feel ugly and unlovable. Cessation of sexual activity due to disease or disability only increases anxiety and loss of self-esteem.

These problems can be compounded by the fact that some people are frightened of illness and disability, just as they are of death, and either avoid the sick or behave in a falsely bright way in their presence. Others may feel it is impolite to talk about ill health and try to cheer the ill person by changing the topic. The ill person may withdraw, fearful of alienating others with constant complaints, resulting in isolation and loneliness. He or she may attempt to stifle feelings of pain or despair out of consideration for family or carers.

CASE HISTORY

'I got polio when I was 21, and I spent six months in an iron lung. I was not expected to live, but I was eventually re-educated to breathe by using other muscles that weren't so wasted by the polio. That was a real shock to the system, somehow; it wasn't that I wanted to die, it was just that I expected to die – and I didn't. I could breathe, but I was still paralysed. It didn't help that nobody could tell me how long I would live, so it was hard to make plans. The first year that I came out of hospital, I became very depressed. It was worst at night, and I actually slept with a razor blade under my pillow – I thought that if it got too bad, I could end it. I remember when I finally came to accept it – it was when I no longer instinctively tried to stand up whenever I felt myself falling from the wheelchair; I had forgotten what that reflex action felt like. I had adjusted to life in a wheelchair, though that didn't mean that other people had adjusted to me being in a wheelchair. They're often quite embarrassed when they first meet me, and I notice that they will always talk to whomever I'm with rather than directly to me (even if it's to ask about me!). Some people become quite patronising, and speak very loudly and slowly, as though I'm a child. It's as though they think weak in the legs means weak in the head. You get used to it, but it hurts.'

Bill, 61, invalid pensioner

COPING WITH DEPRESSION

Not surprisingly, depression is a very common reaction to serious illness and disability. It should not be dismissed as something that has to be 'put up with', but tackled at an early stage, before it becomes entrenched; medical advice should be sought as soon as possible. In the case of sudden illness, the person may seem to cope well through the drama of hospitalisation and rehabilitation, only to become progressively demoralised once back at home, after the medical team which supported him or her through the crisis has withdrawn. Apathy, emotional problems, even breakdown can ensue. These problems may be alleviated to some extent by the strategies outlined in the box below.

In general, however, it is important, as with other forms of grief, that the ill and disabled be allowed to express their emotions and work through their grief. They should be encouraged to realise that it is normal to mourn the impairment of health, and their sorrow should not be invalidated by 'bracing' remarks to the effect that things could be worse, or that so-and-so with the same condition has even more severe problems. Here, once again, professional counselling can help people to work through their grief. A support network of family and friends plays a crucial part in this process. However, sick or disabled people can be very hard to live with, and often the family itself is in need of support.

THINGS THAT MAY HELP

- Depression may be minimised with follow-up care from health professionals.
- Feelings of isolation can be reduced by contact with support groups formed by fellow sufferers.
- Get as much information as possible. Ignorance may be bliss, but it can also lead to baseless fears and needless worry. Anxiety may be reduced if the person knows as much as possible about his condition, including information about future problems and possible outcomes.
- Pain clinics, attached to some major hospitals, can help sufferers of chronic pain to control and come to terms with their condition.
- Sexual counselling may help restore some form of intimacy, perhaps with advice on different positions or techniques. Your doctor may be able to help here, or you could contact RELATE or the British Association for Sexual and Marital Therapy (see pages 99–101).

HELP FOR THE FAMILY

Looking after an ill person can be extremely stressful, particularly if the illness is chronic or terminal. This is not least because such people may feel a great deal of anger at their situation – anger that can be displaced on to the carers.

Mental disorders such as Alzheimer's or schizophrenia can place a special strain on families. They are not only dealing with the hard work of nursing, but may also have to contend with such negative feelings as loneliness, resentment and guilt. They need assistance, reassurance and occasional time out.

Support groups such as the Alzheimer's Disease Society and Schizophrenia Fellowship can help (see page 99). So can advice and counselling from social workers, specialist care nurses and other members of the hospital or community-based health team.

Home care (assistance with nursing, personal care and household tasks) and respite care (in which ill people cared for at home are temporarily accommodated in nursing homes to allow carers to take a holiday) can be a big help.

Ask your doctor, local council or health centre about the availability of such services in your area.

Chapter 10
When a Marriage Ends

It's often said that marriage is taken too lightly nowadays, but divorce is still a major milestone in the lives of most people who experience it. The ending of a marriage almost always provokes deep passions, even if it occurs after only a few weeks. This is because we invest this relationship with such enormous, often unrealistic expectations. We want our partner to give us everything – unconditional love, perfect sex, complete trust and emotional support – denied us in other relationships with family and friends. This 'impossible dream' is shattered when the marriage fails, and the death of this ideal can be the most painful part of the divorce process.

GRIEVING OVER MARRIAGE BREAKDOWN

The end of a marriage provokes the normal grief reactions – denial, anger, bargaining and acceptance – though not everybody necessarily works his or her way through all of them in the same time.

Some experience the first three at once, and remain stuck there. For example, a common example of bargaining is the sudden willingness of a previously reluctant spouse to undergo marriage counselling, long after the other partner has lost interest. Too late to be useful in salvaging the marriage, this behaviour simply signals an unwillingness to recognise that the relationship is over.

Marriages often end with one partner leaving the other for a new person. This usually causes considerable loss of self-esteem for the 'dumped' partner.

The partner who leaves is asserting the power in this situation, so his or her self-esteem is likely to emerge more intact (however much pain may be felt at the time). The partner left behind can further compromise his or her self-esteem by bargaining with the departing spouse – promising to change, to do anything, so long as the partner stays put. By this readiness to change, he or she is in effect putting himself or herself down, implying that his or her present persona is worthless.

DIVORCE DAMAGE

Like other forms of bereavement, the end of a marriage is a major stressor. Partners may stop looking after themselves, which can result in illness.

It's quite common for partners, particularly women, to gain weight as the marriage disintegrates, then lose it rapidly in their new lives alone. This is not so much an attempt to make themselves attractive for a new partner but a symptom of the enormous stress of their changed status.

It is important that you force yourself to eat and sleep properly, to go on holidays and take breaks and so on.

Permit yourself to become a little selfish; don't make the common mistake of thinking you must 'live for your kids' now that the matrimonial relationship has ended. This will only place impossible strains on you and the children.

The stress of divorce can be manifested by unwise life choices. 'Rebound' relationships, selling up and moving away, are common reactions, but should not be undertaken in the first months of grieving, when your ability to think through major decisions is impaired. Change may be inevitable due to changed financial conditions, but should be minimised wherever possible.

Men tend to react worse to the end of a marriage, as their network of emotional support is often less developed than their spouse's. They may rely solely on their wives for emotional sustenance, whereas women seem to be better able, through social conditioning, to express their feelings to others.

TALKING IT THROUGH

As with other forms of bereavement, it helps to work through the pain of divorce by talking it out. This ideally requires a non-judgmental person, one who does not belittle your grief by telling you you'll soon find someone new, or other well-meaning platitudes.

Such perfect listeners can be few and far between, of course, and once again, professional counselling can be very helpful now.

As well as assisting you to identify and work through the grief of marriage breakdown, counselling may also assist you to identify and modify destructive patterns of behaviour that may affect future relationships.

RESOLVING GRIEF

Grieving over marriage breakup is a very individual thing, and some are slower to bounce back than others. On average, the grief tends to be resolved for adults in around two years, though there are no hard and fast rules. Men in particular tend to interrupt the process by forming new relationships, but this is in fact a form of denial and is unlikely to be successful because they may still be programmed into a particular adverse behaviour pattern. Pre-marriage counselling is useful in dispelling unrealistic expectations of marriage; many

CASE HISTORY

'I got married when I was 20, and I really believed that it was until "death do us part". But we were divorced seven years later, after I discovered my husband had been having an affair with another woman.

'It's hard to put into words just how horrible that feeling of betrayal was, particularly since I'd had no inkling beforehand. Richard didn't tell me, but all of a sudden he seemed to have a lot of grudges. I remember him screaming at me that I'd been feeding him cheese on toast for seven years and he'd always hated it!

'When he moved out, I felt as though I had lost my whole existence. One of the most painful moments was opening my own bank account after years of joint accounts; I cried as I filled out the forms. I couldn't sleep, and when I did I had quite violent dreams about Richard and his lover. I kept going over and over what a bastard he was with anyone who would listen. Six months later we had a trial reconciliation, but my heart wasn't in it; I no longer trusted him and we never got back what we had before. It was nothing but fights and rows for the next six months. The actual divorce was the worst time of my life; it really shakes you up in a very fundamental way. I'm just glad we didn't have children. Exposing them to that would have only made me feel more of a failure.'

Deborah, 31, nurse

people find it beneficial before remarrying, to help them avoid repeating the mistakes that destroyed the first marriage.

Money problems are common during and after divorce, and even partners who are determined to remain friendly and civilised can come to blows over property division. Wrangling over home and assets only perpetuates the bitterness of breakup. If you can't agree over who gets what, and you don't wish to proceed to the formal (and often traumatic) process afforded by the law courts, you could be helped by mediation. This is a less intimidating, more low-key procedure in which an impartial third party helps the partners work out a mutually agreeable division of the goods – preventing future anger and resentment.

THE END OF THE AFFAIR

Divorce, however disturbing, at least has the status of a major life event, and a strong grief reaction is expected and tolerated by society. This isn't the case for de facto relationships or lovers who part ways, so their grief can be compounded by not being officially recognised.

The same is true to an even greater degree for gay relationships, whose relationship has even less official existence. It's important to realise that counselling is available (often through traditional marriage guidance and family life centres) for all such relationships.

CHILDREN AND DIVORCE

Spouses aren't the only ones to suffer from the
breakup, of course. Any children of the
marriage are likely to experience intense grief
and anxiety – often more damaging and long-
lasting than that experienced by their parents.

Children's grief reaction can take the form of
misbehaviour at school, or more commonly,
'tuning out' – withdrawing from schoolwork
into their own preoccupations about the
marriage. Young kids can get stuck at the
bargaining stage: telling themselves that if they
are very good, everything might still come
right. Or they may become numb, refusing to
think about the problem at all. Teenagers typically react with anger – anger about the disruption of their lives, or even anger that the
marriage didn't end sooner and stop their
torment.

HOW TO HELP

Children tend to blame themselves, so it's
important to reassure them that the breakup is
not their fault. They should be told that while
Mum and Dad may no longer feel the same
way towards one another as they did, they still
love the child very much.

It helps the child to come to terms with his
grief over the end of the marriage by keeping

him or her in the picture as much as possible. Some people don't think children want to or should know what is going on, but even quite young children can experience anxiety about the future – about where they are to live and with whom, whether there will be enough money to go around, and so forth. The child should be told exactly what is to happen, as calmly as possible. Kids take a pretty black-and-white view of the world and tend to believe someone must be to blame for bad things happening, and it is all too easy for an embittered spouse to turn a child against the other partner. This is understandable, but should be avoided for the child's sake.

Children should be encouraged to show their feelings about the divorce (brace yourself for some devastating honesty). The child should be expected to express his feelings in childish ways, not to react as an adult or as his parents are doing. Very young children are unlikely to come right out and say what is upsetting them, so they could be helped to express their emotions through drawing. This could be done by asking them to make a picture of how they see themselves, their parents and other members of the family and their home.

All these things can be done by grandparents or other relatives as well as the parents. It could be that the parents are too traumatised them-selves to be much help, and once again, profes-sional counselling can help children of divorce.

SELF-HELP CHECKLIST

- Acknowledge and express your pain about the marriage breakdown.
- Seek counselling and mediation if you need help in coping with your feelings or managing the division of property.
- Be cautious about 'rebound relationships' — try to work out where the old marriage went wrong before plunging into another.

HOW TO HELP OTHERS

- Allow separating spouses to express their painful feelings.
- Reassure children of divorce that they are still loved, and not to blame for the breakup. Allow them to say how they feel about the situation.
- Keep children as much in the picture as possible, without encouraging them to side with one spouse against the other.

Chapter 11
Losing Your Job

High levels of unemployment have become a fact of life in the 1990s, and behind every one of those hundreds of thousands of names on the dole queues is a human being in mourning. Losing your job may seem a small thing compared with the death of a loved one, but it can involve money problems, loss of self-esteem, disruption of a familiar routine and possibly relocation, all of which provoke a grief reaction.

Quite apart from the financial implications of getting the sack, that 40-hour week represents an emotional investment second only to our families for many of us. This is because work not only supports us materially, it also gives a sense of common purpose and achievement, a structure to our days, social status and companionship. We define ourselves by our occupations, a fact reflected in the universal question at social introductions: 'What do you do?' In many people's eyes, you are what you do – and if you're no longer doing it, you can suffer a very real loss of your sense of self.

Men tend to take job loss even harder than women, because their whole identity can be based on being the family breadwinner. 'Workaholics' are likely to be harder hit than those with wide interests outside work, or who have a good support network, but very few people are unaffected by the experience.

UNEMPLOYMENT BLUES

Again, as with other forms of bereavement, sacked people typically experience shock, denial, anger and depression. Some can get trapped (at least temporarily) in the denial stage – they don't tell the family, and go off in the morning as though they still had a job. With time, such a person should gradually move towards acceptance of the situation (demonstrated by actively marketing himself for a new job), and the grief should abate with re-employment.

However, it is less likely to be resolved if unemployment proves to be long-term, leading to apathy and feelings of worthlessness. This is a particular problem with young people who have graduated from school straight on to the dole queues, an all-too-common experience in these recessionary times. Confidence and self-esteem take a further battering if the unemployed person makes numerous applications for jobs, only to be met with rejection, or worse, silence. Too many employers fail even to acknowledge applicants' letters.

Unemployed people are unlikely to starve these days, but their health can suffer in other ways. Doctors report increased consultations about stress and anxiety during recessions. Nervous breakdown can follow severance from a long-term occupation, and unemployment is linked with an increased risk of suicide. Depression can be compounded by new-found loneliness and unwanted leisure, as well as the tendency of some people in the community to blame the unemployed for their own plight. In place of a daily kaleidoscope of social contacts – colleagues, customers, even fellow commuters – the unemployed person is socially isolated, stuck at home with only his family for company. They are likely to be as shocked and worried as himself, and the resulting domestic tension only adds to the unemployed person's woes. These can be increased if unemployment leads to other types of loss (moving house, selling the car or other valuables to raise cash, a decline in health or deteriorating relationships). Homelessness or having to apply to charitable organisations for cash or food can be the final straw; the unemployed person can become trapped in a downward spiral of despair and lose all hope and sense of worth.

Unhappily, there aren't likely to be immediate solutions to such problems in a society which places a premium on job status and high salaries, and which still unfairly blames the unemployed for being out of work.

Improvement may only come if people can learn to stop stigmatising the jobless (and the jobless stop stigmatising themselves, however unconsciously).

However, while the long-term unemployed are growing in numbers, they are still the minority and most sacked people will find new employment, if not necessarily as fast as they would like. Losing a job is still a distressing experience, but there are a number of things which you can do to make it a more positive one, and certain strategies to follow which can help minimise some of the destructive aspects of unemployment. Such strategies can commence from the moment of dismissal itself.

ORGANISATIONAL GRIEF

Any kind of upheaval in the workplace causes stress, or what is sometimes called 'organisational grief'. This is all too common in these times of endless corporate takeovers, 'rationalisation', 'downsizing' and all the other euphemisms for the sort of reorganisation that results in retrenchments and job loss, for colleagues if not necessarily yourself. It is worsened if workers are kept in the dark about what is happening. This can cause a host of problems, from petty pilfering to absenteeism and loss of morale, so it is best for employers to be as up front as possible about whatever change is in the offing.

LEARNING FROM THE EXPERIENCE

Many employees take termination personally, asking, 'Why me? Where did I go wrong?' – even when the situation may be beyond their control, as with retrenchment. But being sacked should not equate with personal failure. While job loss is sometimes a result of the employee's inefficiency, more commonly it is caused by company restructuring, being overtaken by new technology or simple bad chemistry. So instead of collapsing in a welter of self-recrimination when you're told to collect your cards, take the time to analyse the situation.

You will have been sacked for one of three reasons:

- inappropriate behaviour on your part (failure to perform as required, inability to co-operate with work mates).
- inappropriate behaviour by others (you are a casualty of insecure superiors, jealous colleagues, a boss who wants your job for a protege).
- external factors (changing job requirements, mergers, the business has gone bust).

There's not a lot you can do about the last two, but if your dismissal was your own fault, try to learn something from the experience. People terminated for bad performance are

SELF-HELP CHECKLIST

Many former pastimes (travel, restaurant meals and so on) will be out of the question if money is short, but most of the following suggestions are inexpensive or free.

- Make a point of getting up at the normal time and dressing properly.
- Get out and about as much as possible; even simple outings like going to the library can help you to feel involved and positive.
- Keep in touch with friends and try to meet new people if you can.
- Take regular exercise and try to watch your diet (at least you've more time for cooking interesting meals now!).
- Investigate retraining schemes and continuing education courses (or simply courses for your own pleasure – if you always wanted to study ancient history or the art of flower arrangement, now's your chance).
- Consider enlisting at a volunteer centre to keep your skills from growing rusty (or to learn new ones).
- Remember that you have an occupation, if a temporarily unpaid one; you are marketing yourself. Develop a job-seeking action plan. Update your curriculum vitae. See if there is a Job Club at your local Job Centre, as well as commercial employment

agencies. Notify your union or professional association that you are available; they often know of unadvertised jobs through the industry pipeline. Target companies you're interested in, and write to the personnel manager, who may well interview you and keep your resume for future reference. At the very least, you'll make new contacts.

- Try to redefine yourself by your attributes and achievements, not by your (paid) occupation. You may not have a job, but you are still a good friend or spouse, gardener or cook or whatever; you are a worthwhile human being.

often astonished because they may not have received any negative feedback up to that point. You need to understand where you went wrong, so ask the person who's firing you why you're being fired. The decision is almost certainly non-negotiable, so don't beg or argue – simply try to get as much information and advice as possible.

KEEPING YOUR COOL

Weeping, threats, even offering violence are common but counter-productive reactions from sacked employees. Keeping calm can be

HOW TO HELP OTHERS

- Don't drop unemployed friends because you are embarrassed by their new status, or no longer feel you can ask them along on expensive outings. Rather, invite them home or on picnics – cheap treats will help them still feel included in a social circle.

- Involve unemployed friends in constructive, collective endeavours (such as building a fence or neighbourhood beautification projects). This can help impart a sense of common purpose and usefulness such as they used to derive from their job.

- If you are an employer who is forced to retrench staff, try not to leave them in the dark until the axe falls. Keep them informed about what is happening, and why.

- If sacking staff for poor performance, take the time to explain (as rationally and constructively as possible) where they went wrong.

- If you are the boss or colleague of a retrenched person, acknowledge his departure with some sort of rite of passage – a special lunch, drinks, and small gift. If, out of embarrassment or misplaced tact, you fail to react as he leaves the office for the last time, it can be very hard on his self-esteem. Keep in touch if possible, so that

> he doesn't feel that he ceased to exist for you as soon as he walked out the door.
> - Try not to equate unemployment with worthlessness. Remember, unemployed people almost always have no choice about their status. They are not lazy, there are simply no longer enough jobs to go around.

difficult, given that bosses don't handle termination any better than employees, but it's essential if you are to salvage anything from the situation. Nobody likes giving bad news, so many bosses simply hand over a cheque and mumble goodbye. But there are ways to turn that painful final interview to your advantage. The important thing to remember is the boss is also feeling vulnerable at this moment, so ask for a reference then, not later. Enquire about severance benefits, retraining programmes, paid time-off to look for another job.

Apart from their obvious practical benefits, all these things allow you to keep some control of the situation, which will help soften the blow to your self-esteem.

KEEPING BUSY

After you've made the best of that final interview, take stock and rebuild your morale.

Sticking to your normal routine (as much as

CASE HISTORY

'I was retrenched four months ago, but it's only recently that I've really started feeling the reaction. I keep going over it in my mind: Why did they do this to me, why did they waste me like this? I could have given them so much.

'What made it worse was that there was nothing personal about it, there was no question of any criticism of my work. It was the old story of a new management moving in, and they wanted their own people in the key positions. It was called "restructuring", but my job was still there, it just had someone else's name on it. It's silly to expect loyalty in business, but it really knocks the stuffing out of you to be treated like that after you've done your best. It was bloody humiliating.

'It's over now, and I know I should try to get on with things and make the best of the job I'm in now, that I started a month ago. But I just can't seem to put it behind me, even though everybody said I was handling it really well at the time. I think that was because I was fighting like mad to get the best redundancy package I could, then after that I was trying to get another job, so I never had a chance to take stock of the situation until now. I don't know if I'll ever really be able to trust an employer again. It's dog eat dog from now on.'

Jim, 36

possible in your altered circumstances) is the anecdote to depression caused by unemployment. Enforced leisure can be disconcerting and demoralising if you're used to being busy all day, with a diary crammed with appointments.

Many of us have no real experience of lots of free time, so we don't really know how to use it constructively when employment ceases. Without a boss telling us what to do, it can become all too easy to slump in front of the television all day. But doing nothing will only increase feelings of boredom and uselessness, further corroding self-esteem. It is important to structure your day with activities, to give a sense of purpose and direction to life.

Helpful Addresses

There are many groups which offer assistance and support to people experiencing bereavement, and a number of these are listed below. You can contact them directly yourself. The head offices listed may be able to put you in touch with a support group in your area, where you can talk to or meet those with a similar experience. In addition the appropriate professional services are listed.

National Association of Bereavement Services
(NABS)
68 Charlton Street
London
NW1 1VR
0171-247 1080
(Telephone helpline answerphone)

National Association of Funeral Directors
618 Warwick Street
Solihull
West Midlands
B91 1AA
0121-711 1343

National Schizophrenia Fellowship
28 Castle Street
Kingston-on-Thames
Surrey
KT1 1SS
0181-974 6814
(Advice line, 10 a.m.–3 p.m. Monday–Friday)

Alzheimer's Disease Society
160 Balham High Road
London
SW12 9BN
0181-675 6557/8/9

British Association for Counselling
1 Regent Place
Rugby
Warwickshire
CV21 2PV
01788 578328

British Association for Sexual and Marital
Therapy
PO Box 62
Sheffield
S10 3TL

Compassionate Friends
53 North Street
Bristol
BS3 1EN

Cruse
126 Sheen Road
Richmond
Surrey
TW9 1UR
0181-332 7227 (Telephone helpline,
9.30 a.m.–5.30 p.m. Monday–Friday)

Disaster Action
11 Lamb Street
London
E1 6EA
0171-377 6691 (Answerphone)

Foundation for the Study of Infant Death
35 Belgrave Square
London
SW1X 8QB
0171-235 1721 (24-hour line)

Miscarriage Association
Clayton Hospital
Northgate, Wakefield
West Yorkshire
WF1 3JS
01924 200799

Missing Persons Helpline
Roebuck House
284-286 Upper Richmond Road West
London
SW14 7JE
0181-392 2000 (24-hour line)

RELATE: National Marriage Guidance
Herbert Gray College
Little Church Street
Rugby
Warwickshire CN21 3AP
01788 573241

SAMARITANS)
Central London Office
46 Marshall Street
London
W1V 1LR
0171-734 2800 (helpline)

Stillbirth and Neonatal Death Society (SANDS)
28 Portland Place
London
W1N 4DE
0171-436 5881

ROBINSON FAMILY HEALTH

All your health questions answered in a way you really understand.

Titles available from booksellers or direct from Robinson include:

Arthritis: What *Really* Works
Dava Sobel & Arthur C. Klein
1–85487–290–7   £7.99

Asthma
Megan Gressor
1–85487–386–5   £2.99

Bad Backs: A Self-Help Guide
Leila Henderson
1–85487–388–1   £2.99

Bulimia Nervosa and Binge-Eating
Dr Peter Cooper
1–85487–171–4   £6.99

Headaches: Relief at Last
Megan Gressor
1–85487–391–1   £2.99

Let's Get Things Moving: Overcoming Constipation
Pauline Chiarelli and Sue Markwell
1–85487–389–X   £2.99

Living With Loss & Grief
Geoffrey Glassock and Megan Gressor
1–85487–384–9   £2.99

Massage for Common Ailments
Penny Rich
Illustrated in full colour
1–85487–306–7   £4.99

Menopause Made Easy
Kendra Sundquist
1–85487–389–X   £2.99

Pregnancy and Birth
Kerrie Lee
1–85487–390–3   £2.99

Treating IBS
Dr Christine P. Dancey & Susan Backhouse
1–85487–314–8   £6.99

Practical Aromatherapy
Penny Rich
Illustrated in full colour
1–85487–315–6   £4.99

**The Recovery Book: A Self-Help Guide for
Recovering Alcoholics, Addicts and Their Families**
Al J. Mooney, Arlene Eisenberg & Howard Eisenberg
1–85487–292–3   £9.99

Women's Waterworks
Pauline Chiarelli
1–85487–382–2   £2.99

You *Can* Beat Period Pain
Liz Kelly
1–85487–381–4   £2.99

Your Baby: The First 12 Months
Lynda Wilton
1–85487–387–3   £2.99

How to Order

To order a book, please send a cheque (made
out to Robinson Publishing Ltd) or postal order
to the address below, adding 50p per title for

postage and packing. Send to: **Family Health, Robinson Publishing Ltd, 7 Kensington Church Court, London W8 4SP.**

While this information was correct at the time of going to press, details may change without notice.